WHAT I SEE IN SUMMER

by Danielle J. Jacks

TABLE OF CONTENTS

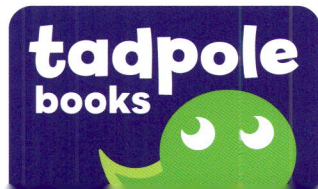

tadpole books

WORDS TO KNOW

butterfly

grass

picnic

pool

sunflowers

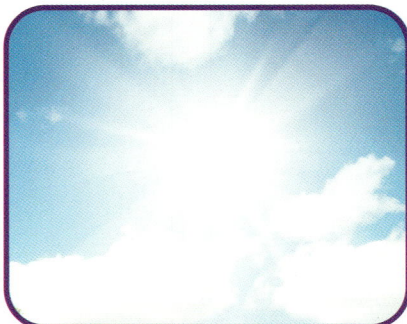

sunshine

WHAT I SEE IN SUMMER

I see sunshine!

3

grass

I see grass.

sunflower

I see sunflowers.

I see a picnic.

butterfly

I see a butterfly.

pool

I see a pool.

I see a ball.

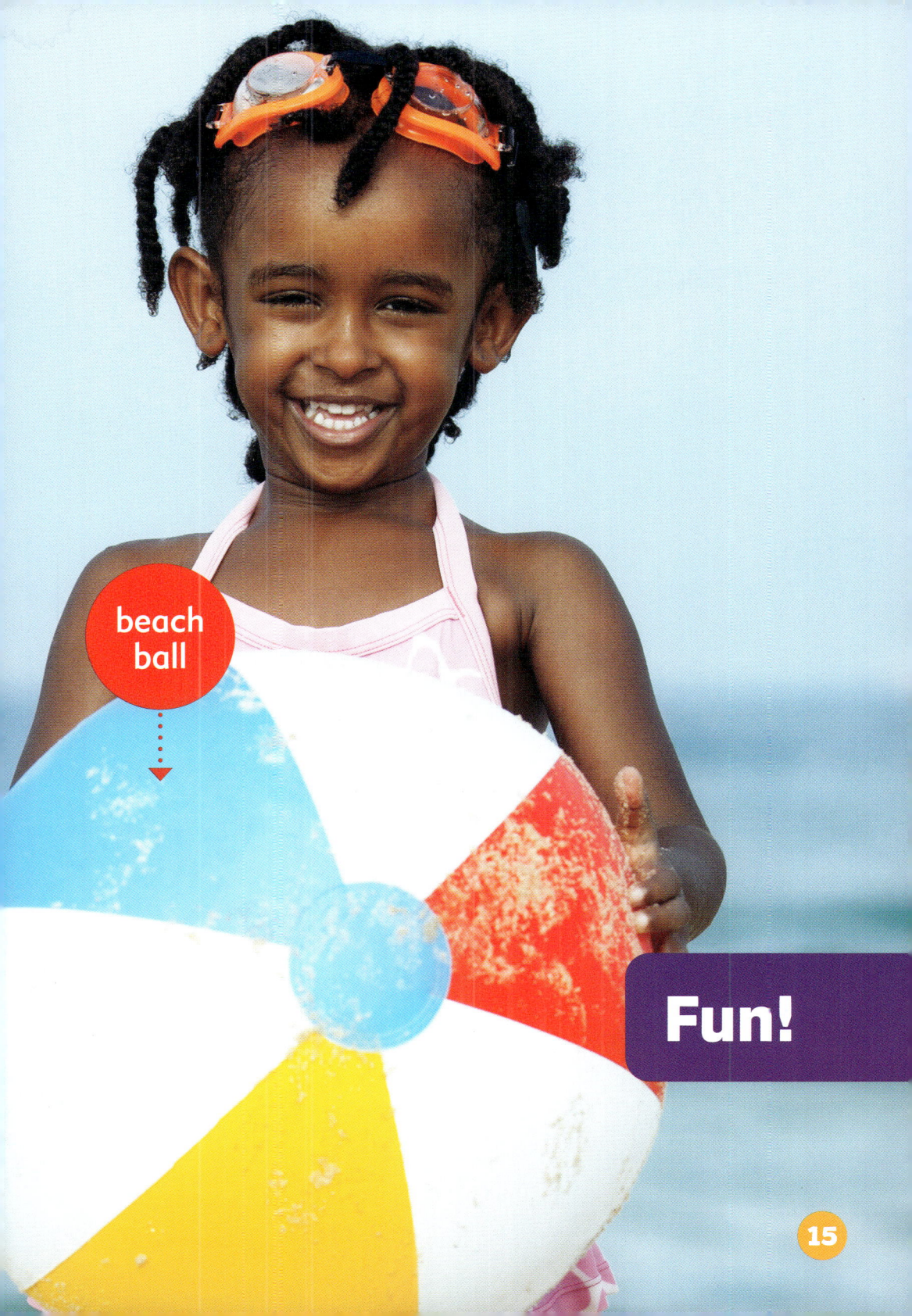

beach
ball

Fun!

LET'S REVIEW!

What are these kids doing in summer?

INDEX